S0-AUZ-716

American Holidays / Celebraciones en los Estados Unidos

COLUMBUS DAY
DÍA DE LA RAZA

Connor Dayton Traducción al español: Eduardo Alamán

PowerKiDS press
New York

Published in 2012 by The Rosen Publishing Group, Inc.
29 East 21st Street, New York, NY 10010

First Edition

Editor: Jennifer Way
Book Design: Julio Gil

Traducción al español: Eduardo Alamán

Photo Credits: Cover, p. 21 Spencer Platt/Getty Images; pp. 5, 24 (top left) SuperStock/Getty Images; p. 7 Shutterstock.com; p. 9 Universal History Archive/Getty Images; pp. 11, 24 (bottom) Kean Collection/Getty Images; p. 13 Apic/Getty Images; p. 15 Photos.com/Thinkstock; p. 17 Timothy A. Clary/AFP/Getty Images; pp. 19, 23, 24 (top right) Mario Tama/Getty Images.

Library of Congress Cataloging-in-Publication Data

Dayton, Connor.
[Columbus Day. Spanish & English]
Columbus Day = Día de la Raza / by Connor Dayton. — 1st ed.
p. cm. — (American holidays = Celebraciones en los Estados Unidos)
Includes index.
ISBN 978-1-4488-6711-0 (library binding)
1. Columbus Day—Juvenile literature. 2. Columbus, Christopher—Juvenile literature. 3. America—Discovery and exploration—Spanish—Juvenile literature. I. Title. II. Title: Día de la Raza.
E120.D3918 2012
394.264—dc23

2011027090

Web Sites: Due to the changing nature of Internet links, PowerKids Press has developed an online list of Web sites related to the subject of this book. This site is updated regularly. Please use this link to access the list: www.powerkidslinks.com/amh/columbus/

Manufactured in the United States of America

CPSIA Compliance Information: Batch #WW12PK: For Further Information contact Rosen Publishing, New York, New York at 1-800-237-9932

Contents

Contenido

Columbus Day honors the **explorer** Christopher Columbus.

El Día de la Raza honra al **explorador** Cristóbal Colón.

COLVMBI. ANTIPODVM. PRIMV
ORBEM

Columbus was from Genoa, in today's Italy.

Colón nació en Génova, en lo que hoy es Italia.

Switzerland
Suiza
Slovenia
Eslovenia
Croatia
Croacia
Bosnia -
Herzegovina
Boznia-
Herzegovina
Genoa
Génova
Italy
Italia
France
Francia
Montenegro
Montenegro
Adriatic Sea
Mar Adriático
Corsica
Córcega
Tyrrhenian Sea
Mar Tirreno
Sicily
Sicilia
Sardinia
Cerdeña

In 1492, Columbus sailed from Spain. He wanted to get to India by crossing the Atlantic Ocean.

En 1492, Colón navegó desde España. Colón quería encontrar India cruzando el océano Atlántico.

Columbus had three **ships**. They were the *Niña*, the *Pinta*, and the *Santa María*.

Colón tenía tres **barcos**: la *Niña*, la *Pinta* y la *Santa María*.

Columbus saw land on October 12, 1492. He thought he had reached Asia.

Colón tocó tierra el 12 de octubre de 1492. Colón pensó que había llegado a Asia.

He called these islands the West Indies. He called the people Indians.

Colón llamó a estas tierras las Indias Occidentales. Colón llamó indios a sus habitantes.

Columbus Day is the second Monday in October.

El Día de la Raza se celebra el segundo lunes de octubre.

Columbus Day **parades** honor both the explorer and Italian Americans.

El Día de la Raza honra con **desfiles** a Colón y a los italoamericanos.

ITALIAN - ENGLISH
DUAL LANGUAGE
PROGRAM
BUSES
& RIGHT TURNS
ONLY
7AM-7PM
MON THRU FRI
ITALIAN - ENGLISH
DUAL LANGUAGE PROGRAM
JEFFERSON ELEMENTARY SCHOOL
NEW ROCHELLE, N.Y.

New York City has the biggest Columbus Day parade.

El desfile más grande del Día de la Raza se celebra en Nueva York.

24

What do you do on Columbus Day?

¿Qué haces el Día de la Raza?

Words to Know / Palabras que debes saber

explorer / (el) explorador

parade / (el) desfile

ships / (los) barcos

Index

Índice